Special Spoonfuls!

A Delightful New Way To Give A Food Mix!
Give decorated plastic spoons full of dip mixes, cheeseball
mixes, drink mixes. The recipient stirs the mix from the
spoon into sour cream, water . . to make a delicious treat!
Jackie Gannaway

Published in Austin, TX by COOKBOOK CUPBOARD
P.O. Box 50053, Austin, TX 78763 (512) 477-7070 phone   (512) 891-0094 fax

ISBN 1-885597-41-X

Artwork by Frank Bielec of Mosey 'N Me-Katy, TX.

Over 1.5 Million Copies Of Jackie Gannaway's Books Are In Print!

This book is part of
"Jackie's Originals Collection-
Creative New Concepts in Gift Mixes™"

Jackie Gannaway

Mail Order Information
To order a copy of this book send a check for $3.95 + $1.50 for shipping (TX residents add 8.25 % sales tax) to Cookbook Cupboard, P.O. Box 50053, Austin, TX 78763. Send a note asking for this title by name. If you would like a descriptive list of the nearly 40 fun titles in The Kitchen Crafts Collection and The Layers of Love Collection™ and Jackie's Originals Collection - Creative New Concepts in Gift Mixes™ send a note, call or fax (numbers at top of this page) asking for a brochure.

What Is This Book About?

This book has recipes for gift mixes to attach to colorful plastic spoons. There are spoon mix recipes for hot flavored cocoas, teas, and coffees, dessert cheeseballs, fruit dips and spreads, mousse, spicy dips, butters and salad dressing. The hot drink mixes make an individual serving. In the other recipes, the spoon mix makes four servings.

The mix is wrapped in plastic wrap, placed in the bowl part of a plastic spoon and secured by taping it to the base of the spoon handle. The mix is covered by tissue paper, cellophane or fabric - and tied with a decorative tie. Instructions are written on a card and attached to the spoon. There are endless decorating and personalizing possibilities. (Paint greetings or names on spoon handle with paint pens, for example.)

These are nice gifts by themselves, or as part of a gift basket. Following are many examples and decorating ideas. (Recipe list - see Index -pg.32)

As with all good gift mix recipes these are simple for you to make and also simple for the recipient. The recipes use only a few ingredients and those ingredients are everyday ordinary ingredients. These spoon gift mixes are very inexpensive to make.

It will be helpful to read all the introductory pages in this book before making spoon mixes. Many ideas and suggestions are given.

General Procedure For Making The Mix

At the top of each page is the recipe for the mix you are going to give. It is called "--------- Spoonful Mix". Each recipe is written for making one mix at a time. In theory you could quadruple the single recipe in a bowl, then scoop out the amount you need for each mix, but in practice that doesn't work well. The reason is that the heavier ingredients (salt, sugar) tend to fall to the bottom of the mixing bowl and aren't scooped up equally with the lighter ingredients (dillweed, parsley flakes) - so the last mix you scoop from the bowl will have all the salt and sugar and the first mixes won't. The flavors won't be the same from mix to mix.

Work out an assembly line with the ingredients, measuring spoons, plastic wrap, spoons and tape in front of you. Mix one mix, wrap it in plastic wrap, attach it to the spoon. Repeat until you have made all the spoons you need. Decorate spoons assembly line fashion.

Measurement Notes: For the mixes that use gelatin or pudding as an ingredient here are the amounts of Tb. and tsp. in each box to help you know how many boxes to buy for the number of mixes you want to make:

4 serving size of sugar free gelatin mix: 3 tsp.
4 serving size of gelatin mix with sugar: 17 to 19 tsp. or 5 to 6 Tb.
(Amount varies by brand name.)
4 serving size instant pudding mix (not sugar free): 6 to 8 Tb.
(Amount varies by brand name.)

How Will The Recipient Use The Mix

The recipient will use this mix to make a drink, a dip or spread, a mousse, a flavored butter, a dessert cheeseball, a salad dressing.

She will read the instruction card you include (the words you use for the instructions are printed on each page below the recipe for the mix).

This will tell her to place the necessary ingredient (such as sour cream) into a bowl. She will remove the decorations from the spoon and snip the plastic wrap holding the mix with a sharp knife or scissors and allow the mix to fall into the bowl with the sour cream. In some cases she can even use the gift spoon to stir the mix (in other cases such as mixing cream cheese - she will have to use a sturdy mixing spoon from her kitchen).

What Kind Of Spoon?

Use heavyweight plastic spoons in white, clear or a color that is appropriate to the theme of the gift (Christmas, Easter, Birthday, Wedding or Wedding Shower). Plan how you will decorate the spoons before choosing a color. Buy a pack of spoons at party supply stores, crafts stores or grocery stores. Boxes of 500 white spoons are available Sam's Club or Costco for just over a penny each.

For extra special gifts use antique silverplate spoons. Mismatched spoons cost $1 to $2 each at antique stores and flea markets.

How To Attach The Mix To The Spoon
Using Sandwich Bags

Use a fold and close sandwich bag (not a zipper sandwich bag). Cut sandwich bag in half with scissors. Each half will be a little "pouch" for the dry mix. Place the mix in the pouch, twist it closed and tape it closed with tape. (It will be the shape of a strawberry, with the corner of the sandwich bag looking like the tip end of the strawberry.)

Tape bag to the handle of the spoon with mix sitting in the bowl part of the spoon. Don't tape the entire surface of the bag of mix to spoon - that will make it difficult for the recipient to get the mix out of the bag.

Using Plastic Wrap

Use a 5" square of plastic wrap (clear or colored). (It doesn't have to be measured with a ruler - you will quickly see what size you need.) Cut plastic wrap into squares with scissors. Place the mix in the middle of the square. Bring up the sides of the square, Twist this into a little bag. Tape the bag closed and attach to the spoon as described above. (Cut away any excess plastic wrap.)

Decorating The Spoon Mixes

Your objective is to tie a decorative covering over the mix so the bowl of the spoon is colorfully decorated.

How To Cover The Mix

Cut covering material into an 8" square. (Can fold square into quarters and cut it into a circle, but that is not really necessary - the finished look won't be much different whether you start with a square or a circle.) But it definitely has to be 8" to give a full, attractive covering.

Place the spoon of mix into the center of this 8" square and fold up the corners completely enclosing the bowl part of the spoon. Twist this tight against the base of the spoon handle and place a tight piece of tape around this place. Add a decorative tie (see pg. 6).

Covering Materials To Use

Tissue Paper - Solid color or printed. (Use college print tissue for sending spoons to a person away at college.)

(I noticed a surprising thing when I was decorating spoons - colored tissue paper looked very good on a single spoon- but when I made "sets" with a bowl or a plate and 4 to 6 spoons all decorated to match a theme - I found that tissue paper looked drab. When I changed to colored cellophane in those instances, the look was much more festive.)

cont'd on pg.5   4

cont'd from pg. 4

Cellophane - This is available in rolls (clear and many colors) at crafts stores. It has a nice festive sheen to it. (Don't use the clear for covering the mix - the mix will still be visible.)

10" paper doilies in white, colors, gold or silver. 10" sounds too large but other sizes won't cover the mix.

Fabric - Any kind of fabric or all-over lace can be used. Use holiday printed fabrics - coordinate the color of fabric to color of the spoon. Match tie with the type of fabric (raffia with bandana fabric, silk ribbon with eyelet fabric). To use fabric as a covering, cut a piece 3 1/2" x 9". Use pinking shears if desired. Fold fabric over spoon mix as described below for wide ribbon.

Wide Ribbon - Use a 10" length of 2 1/2" to 3" wide ribbon - specifically the kind of ribbon with printed designs. There are designs for every theme and occasion. Fold ribbon in half crosswise. Place spoon mix in the center of the ribbon and tie ribbon closed with a decorative tie. The edges of the ribbon are open, but the ribbon is wide enough that the mix can't be seen.

Printed paper napkins- Party napkins come in many designs. They work well as coverings for spoons. Experiment with unfolding them all the way, half the way, etc. until they work best as a covering.

 ## Unusual Coverings To Use

Plastic fillable Easter eggs - Everyone is familiar with fillable plastic Easter eggs - they are egg sized and come in many colors. They separate in the middle to be filled - then snap back together. Many of these eggs are made of a soft enough plastic that a steak knife can make a slit in the top of the fat half. The handle of the spoon can be inserted through the slit and then the other part of the egg can be attached, encasing the mix inside the egg with the handle sticking out of the top of the egg. Sometimes a little hot glue is necessary at the place where the handle enters the egg to keep it tight. Tie a bow around the handle, put stickers on the plastic egg, put a lace "skirt" on the egg - anything you can think of.

Clear fillable plastic balls - These are balls the size of Christmas ornaments designed to be filled with potpourri, etc. They are available at crafts stores. Since they are clear and the mix can be seen inside them, fill them with the appropriate color of Easter grass. Put the mix spoon inside the grass. Carefully place the halves of the ball back together around the spoon allowing the handle to come out the top. Use tape to tape the ball halves together securely. (The tape won't show on the clear ball, especially because the grass is showing through the ball.) Add decorative ribbons to the place where the handle comes out of the ball.

Styrofoam cups with lids- These are perfect for giving a drink mix spoon. Look at grocery stores for 12 oz. styrofoam cups with lids (you might have to go to a restaurant supply store). Decorate the cup with a paint pen - write the recipients name on the cup (kids can do this), add stickers - place the undecorated drink mix spoon into the cup - cut a slit in the lid for the spoon handle. Tie a bow around where the handle enters the cup. Either give it like that or wrap cellophane or tissue around the entire thing and add a bow.

This is a perfect little gift for co-workers because all they need to add is boiling water (if there is a microwave- they can enjoy your gift right at the office). 5

Ties To Use

Curling ribbon, regular ribbon, fancy ribbon - The covering you choose will look good with ribbon - decide which type of ribbon goes best with your covering. Use plain tissue paper with several different colors of curling ribbon all tied and curled. Use 1" wide satin ribbon and glue on a small silk flower. It takes a 20" length of ribbon to make a bow on a spoon mix.

Chenille stems - These are 12" long fuzzy wires (crafts stores). Use the entire length and form a bow or wrap the ends around a pencil for a spiral look. Or cut the stem in half and use it to tie two spoons. I like the metallic chenille stems best, but you will see which kind and color goes best with your decoration theme.

Wired star garlands- These are sold in the gift wrap aisle. They come in many colors. Cut garland into 6" lengths for ties.

Raffia - (Crafts stores) - Comes in tan or colors. It gives a rougher look for western or country style decorations.

Additional Decorations

At this point your spoon is finished enough, but you can continue to add decorations such as a small silk flower, a "skirt" of 3" wide pre-gathered lace, a jingle bell or other seasonal decoration. Anything that is the right size and can be hot-glued will work. You can really get a specific theme by gluing on ornamentation.

Read "*Spoon Specialties*" throughout this book - they list many good ideas including making "sets" with a matching bowl or plate (for serving the cheeseball or the dip), adding a matching plastic knife (to be the butter knife for a flavored butter mix), placing several decorated spoons into a paper towel roll and wrapping the roll with cellophane, placing a dip or salad dressing mix into a full size wooden spoon instead of a plastic spoon. (Good as part of a basket for a kitchen shower.)

Paint Pen Greetings

Use a paint pen (crafts store) to write a greeting or to write the name of the mix along the spoon handle. To teachers from children, to co-workers and bridge club members - as a fundraiser for the team. Write the appropriate words on the spoon handle in a coordinating color of paint pen.

Recipe Cards

Attach a recipe card to the spoon telling how to use the mix. The words you use are in a plain box on each page of this book. Type these words into your computer and print out on heavy paper. Add computer clip art or add stickers or your own calligraphy or artwork. Let your kids decorate the recipe card. Punch a hole in the corner of the card and tie it onto the spoon with ribbon.

You might choose to make the card long and skinny instead of rectangular - that way you can tape it to the back side of the spoon handle.

Look through your crafts, sewing and gift wrap supplies. You already have many things to use to decorate these spoon mixes. If you have a theme in mind for a specific occasion it is fun to wander through a store that sells both fabrics and crafts (Pacific Fabrics, Hobby Lobby, Wal-Mart) to see what is available and to coordinate everything. Have fun with this simple idea. Jackie Gannaway

Milk Shakers
Spoonful Mix

1 Tb. + 1 tsp. instant pudding mix (not sugar free)

Choose one of these flavors: Vanilla, White Chocolate, Lemon, Butterscotch, Banana Cream, Cheesecake.

Don't use Coconut Cream, Pistachio or any of the chocolate flavors. Coconut and pistachio have crystals and nuts that aren't good in a drink - chocolate is not an unusual flavor for milk - use something unusual).

1. Place mix into plastic wrap and attach to spoon.
   Decorate spoon. Attach instructions below.
   Name it for whichever flavor you are using.
   (See pgs. 3-6 for detailed instructions on this.)

Banana Milk Shaker

1. Remove decorative wrapping from spoon, leaving the mix inside the plastic wrap and still attached to spoon.
2. Place one cup (8 oz.) milk into a small plastic container with a lid.
3. Hold spoon over milk. Cut open bag of mix, allowing mix to fall into milk.
4. Put lid on container and shake 30 seconds. Drink immediately.

NOTE: To make a hot drink, shake up milk and then place it into a microsafe mug. Microwave 30 to 45 seconds.

Spoon Specialties

Buy a childs plastic drinking glass with a lid and a built-in straw. These are available at discount stores and general merchandise stores. They cost between 89¢ and $3.00. This gift can be very inexpensive with the 89¢ glass. Give a glass and some milk shaker spoons. The recipient can shake the milk shakers right in the little glass.

Write the names of each flavor on the handle of each spoon with a paint pen.

Sweet and Smooth Dessert Cheeseball
Spoonful Mix

1 1/2 Tb. white chocolate instant pudding mix (not sugar free)

1 1/2 Tb. Amaretto flavor powdered coffee creamer

1. Mix both ingredients in small bowl.
2. Place mix into plastic wrap and attach to spoon. Decorate spoon. Attach instructions below. (See pgs. 3-6 for detailed instructions on this.)

Sweet and Smooth
Dessert Cheeseball

1. Remove decorative wrapping from spoon, leaving the mix inside the plastic wrap and still attached to spoon.
2. Place **1 (8 oz.) block cream cheese**, room temperature, into a medium bowl.
3. Hold spoon over bowl and cut open bag of mix, allowing mix to fall into bowl onto cream cheese.
4. Mix until very well blended. Shape into a ball. Store in refrigerator, but serve at room temperature.
5. Serve with strawberries, green grapes, banana slices or small shortbread cookies.

Spoon Specialties

A Complete Pasta Dinner From Spoons!

Place spoons in a gift basket for Parmesan Herb Pasta Butter (pg. 22), Ranch Dressing (pg. 32), Garlic Butter (pg. 31), this dessert cheeseball mix, a 6 oz. or 12 oz. package of spaghetti, a loaf of Italian bread and a bottle of wine.

Include a note listing the menu and their grocery list. Their grocery list is butter, buttermilk, mayo, bag of salad, 8 oz. block cream cheese, fresh strawberries.

Those groceries, plus what you are giving them in the basket, makes a complete dinner for four.

Milk Chocolate or Mocha Dessert Cheeseball Spoonful Mix

1 1/2 Tb. sugar
1 Tb. Nesquik® chocolate drink mix
1/2 tsp. instant coffee granules (optional - include it if
 you want mocha flavor)

1. Mix all ingredients in small bowl.
2. Place mix into plastic wrap and attach to spoon.
 Decorate spoon. Attach instructions below.
 (See pgs. 3-6 for detailed instructions on this.)
 Name it either "Milk Chocolate" or "Mocha" depending
 on which flavor you are using.

Milk Chocolate Dessert Cheeseball

1. Remove decorative wrapping from spoon, leaving the
 mix inside the plastic wrap and still attached to spoon.
2. Place **1 (8 oz.) block cream cheese**, room temperature, into a medium bowl.
3. Hold spoon over bowl and cut open bag of mix, allowing
 mix to fall into bowl onto cream cheese.
4. Mix until very well blended. Shape into a ball. Store in
 refrigerator, but serve at room temperature.
5. Serve with strawberries, green grapes, banana slices or
 small shortbread cookies.

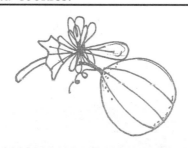

Spoon Specialties

 Give this mix in a gift basket with some fruit if they
will eat it right away or with some small fancy shortbread
cookies. Include a matching plastic knife for spreading
the cheeseball, and some matching paper napkins.

Confetti Dessert Cheeseball
Spoonful Mix

1 Tb. flaked coconut
2 tsp. finely chopped pecans
2 tsp. sugar
2 tsp. pineapple gelatin mix (not sugar free)
1/2 tsp. cherry gelatin mix (not sugar free)

1. Mix all ingredients in small bowl.
2. Place mix into plastic wrap and attach to spoon.
   Decorate spoon. Attach instructions below.
   (See pgs. 3-6 for detailed instructions on this.)

Confetti Dessert Cheeseball

1. Remove decorative wrapping from spoon, leaving the
   mix inside the plastic wrap and still attached to spoon.
2. Place **1 (8 oz.) block cream cheese**, room temperature, into a medium bowl.
3. Hold spoon over bowl and cut open bag of mix, allowing
   mix to fall into bowl onto cream cheese.
4. Mix until very well blended. Shape into a ball. Store in
   refrigerator, but serve at room temperature.
5. Serve with strawberries, green grapes, banana slices or
   small shortbread cookies.

Spoon Specialties

   Make a matching serving "set" by placing the cheeseball spoon onto a matching plastic plate (this will be the
serving plate for the cheeseball). Include 4 matching
paper napkins and a plastic knife. Place the napkins on
the plate first, then the spoon and knife. The party section
of the crafts store or a party supply store has all colors of
plastic party ware. Tie all this up with clear cellophane
and a bow.

Lemon* Cream Cheese
Spread For Bagels Or Fruit
Spoonful Mix

2 1/2 Tb. lemon gelatin mix (not sugar free)

1. Place gelatin mix into plastic wrap and attach to spoon. Decorate spoon. Attach instructions below. (See pgs. 3-6 for detailed instructions on this.)

*NOTE: Use another flavor of gelatin mix, such as orange, strawberry, cherry or pineapple for a different flavor. Name it for the flavor you are using.

Lemon Cream Cheese Spread

1. Remove decorative wrapping from spoon, leaving the mix inside the plastic wrap and still attached to spoon.
2. Empty **1 (8 oz.) tub soft cream cheese**, room temperature, into a medium bowl.
3. Hold spoon over bowl and cut open bag of mix, allowing mix to fall into bowl onto cream cheese.
4. Mix until very well blended. Store in refrigerator, but serve at room temperature.
5. Serve with strawberries, green grapes, banana slices or small shortbread cookies. Use as a spread for bagels.

Spoon Specialties

Breakfast Basket

Give a Lemon Cream Cheese Spread Spoon in a basket with bagels and a few drink mix spoons (pgs. 16-22).

Cinnamon Fruit Dip
Spoonful Mix

2 Tb. brown sugar
2 tsp. lemon gelatin mix (not sugar free)
1/2 tsp. cinnamon
1/2 tsp. nutmeg
1/4 tsp. ground ginger

1. Mix all ingredients in small bowl.
2. Place mix into plastic wrap and attach to spoon.
   Decorate spoon. Attach instructions below.
   (See pgs. 3-6 for detailed instructions on this.)

Cinnamon Fruit Dip

1. Remove decorative wrapping from spoon, leaving the
   mix inside the plastic wrap and still attached to spoon.
2. Place **1 cup (8 oz.) sour cream** into a medium bowl.
3. Hold spoon over bowl and cut open bag of mix, allowing
   mix to fall into bowl onto sour cream.
4. Mix until very well blended. (Use gift spoon to mix!)
   Store in refrigerator.
5. Serve with strawberries, seedless green grapes, banana
   slices, apple slices or small shortbread cookies.

Spoon Specialties

Decorated spoons are very colorful. Put several
different dip spoons (pg. 12-14 and 23-27) in a gallon size
plastic freezer bag. Decorate the spoons differently from
each other, but in a coordinating way. Cut off the zipper
part of the bag and tie bag shut with ribbons that match
the decor of the spoons inside the bag.

Orange, Raspberry or Strawberry Fruit Dip Spoonful Mix

2 Tb. brown sugar
2 tsp. orange, raspberry or strawberry gelatin mix (not
   sugar free)

1. Mix all ingredients in small bowl.
2. Place mix into plastic wrap and attach to spoon.
   Decorate spoon. Attach instructions below.
   Name it for the flavor you are using.
   (See pgs. 3-6 for detailed instructions on this.)

Orange Fruit Dip

1. Remove decorative wrapping from spoon, leaving the
   mix inside the plastic wrap and still attached to spoon.
2. Place **1 cup (8 oz.) sour cream** into a medium bowl.
3. Hold spoon over bowl and cut open bag of mix, allowing
   mix to fall into bowl onto sour cream.
4. Mix until very well blended. (Use gift spoon to mix!)
   Store in refrigerator.
5. Serve with strawberries, seedless green grapes, banana
   slices or small shortbread cookies.

Spoon *Specialties*

   Get a plastic bowl (permanent or disposable) or a
ceramic bowl that holds about 3 cups. Place 6 different
dip spoons (pgs. 12-14 and 23-27) in the bowl. This will be
the bowl the dip is served in. Wrap everything with
cellophane and tie with a bow.

Ginger Spread
Spoonful Mix

2 Tb. sugar
1/2 tsp. cinnamon
1/2 tsp. ground ginger
1/4 tsp. nutmeg

1. Mix all ingredients in small bowl.
2. Place mix into plastic wrap and attach to spoon. Decorate spoon. Attach instructions below. (See pgs. 3-6 for detailed instructions on this.)

Ginger Spread

1. Remove decorative wrapping from spoon, leaving the mix inside the plastic wrap and still attached to spoon.
2. Place **1 (8 oz.) block cream cheese**, room temperature, into a medium bowl.
3. Hold spoon over bowl and cut open bag of mix, allowing mix to fall into bowl onto cream cheese.
4. Mix until very well blended.
5. Serve with sliced fruit or small shortbread or gingersnaps cookies. Store in refrigerator, but serve at room temperature.

Dip For Apples
Spoonful Mix

2 Tb. brown sugar
1 Tb. vanilla powder (spice section or coffee section of store or at gourmet stores)

1. Mix all ingredients in small bowl.
2. Place mix into plastic wrap and attach to spoon. Decorate spoon. Attach instructions at top of pg. 15. (See pgs. 3-6 for detailed instructions on this.) Give with some apples for dipping, if desired.

14

Dip For Apples

1. Remove decorative wrapping from spoon, leaving the mix inside the plastic wrap and still attached to spoon.
2. Empty **1 (8 oz.) tub soft cream cheese**, room temp., into medium bowl.
3. Hold spoon over bowl and cut open bag of mix, allowing mix to fall into bowl onto cream cheese.
4. Mix until very well blended. Store in refrigerator, but serve at room temp.
5. Serve with apple slices.

Lemon, Orange or Chocolate Mousse Spoonful Mix

For lemon or orange:
2 Tb. lemon instant pudding mix (not sugar free)
2 tsp. sugar free lemon or orange gelatin mix

For chocolate:
2 Tb. chocolate fudge instant pudding mix
2 tsp. Nesquick® chocolate flavored drink mix

1. Mix all ingredients in small bowl.
2. Place mix into plastic wrap and attach to spoon.
   Decorate spoon. Attach instructions below.
   Name it for flavor you are using.
   (See pgs. 3-6 for detailed instructions on this.)

Chocolate Mousse

1. Remove decorative wrapping from spoon, leaving the mix inside the plastic wrap and still attached to spoon.
2. Empty **1 (8 oz.) tub frozen whipped topping, thawed** into medium bowl.
3. Hold spoon over bowl and cut open bag of mix, allowing mix to fall into bowl onto whipped topping.
4. Mix until very well blended. (Use gift spoon to mix!)
   Store in refrigerator. Serve chilled.

Cinnamon, Raspberry Or Orange Cocoa Spoonful Mix

1 Tb. Nesquik® chocolate flavored drink mix
2 Tb. vanilla flavor powdered coffee creamer
1/2 tsp. cinnamon OR 1/2 tsp. raspberry gelatin or orange
  gelatin (not sugar free)

1. Mix all ingredients in small bowl.
2. Place mix into plastic wrap and attach to spoon.
   Decorate spoon. Attach instructions below.
   Name it for the flavor you are using.
   (See pgs. 3-6 for detailed instructions on this.)

Cinnamon Cocoa

1. Remove decorative wrapping from spoon, leaving the
   mix inside the plastic wrap and still attached to spoon.
2. Hold spoon over a mug and cut open bag of mix, allowing
   mix to fall into mug.
3. Add one cup (8 oz.) boiling water.
4. Stir until well mixed. (Use gift spoon to stir!)

Spoon Specialties

Give 6 spoonfuls of this cocoa mix in a gift basket with
a zipper bag of mini marshmallows. Tie ribbons on the bag
of mini marshmallows. Include 2 mugs if desired.

Cinnamon Coffee
Spoonful Mix

2 1/2 tsp. sugar
1 1/2 tsp. vanilla flavor powdered coffee creamer
1/2 tsp. instant coffee granules
1/4 tsp. cinnamon

1. Mix all ingredients in small bowl.
2. Place mix into plastic wrap and attach to spoon.
   Decorate spoon. Attach instructions below.
   (See pgs. 3-6 for detailed instructions on this.)

Cinnamon Coffee

1. Remove decorative wrapping from spoon, leaving the
   mix inside the plastic wrap and still attached to spoon.
2. Hold spoon over a mug and cut open bag of mix, allowing
   mix to fall into mug.
3. Add one cup (8 oz.) boiling water.
4. Stir until well mixed. (Use gift spoon to stir!)

Spoon   *Specialties*

Place several different flavors of drink spoons (pgs. 16 to 22) into a ceramic mug. Wrap whole thing with cellophane. Tie with ribbons.

Russian Tea
Spoonful Mix

1 1/2 tsp. orange flavored breakfast drink mix (like Tang®)
1 1/2 tsp. Country Time® lemonade powder (not sugar free)
1 tsp. unsweetened instant tea
1 tsp. sugar
1/2 tsp. cinnamon
1/4 tsp. nutmeg
1/4 tsp. ground ginger

1. Mix all ingredients in small bowl.
2. Place mix into plastic wrap and attach to spoon.
   Decorate spoon. Attach instructions below.
   (See pgs. 3-6 for detailed instructions on this.)

Russian Tea

1. Remove decorative wrapping from spoon, leaving the
   mix inside the plastic wrap and still attached to spoon.
2. Hold spoon over a mug and cut open bag of mix, allowing
   mix to fall into mug.
3. Add one cup (8 oz.) boiling water.
4. Stir until well mixed. (Use gift spoon to stir!)

Spoon *Specialties*

Give a spoon of Russian Tea with a china teacup and
saucer (discount store, flea market). Instead of a plastic
spoon, buy a silverplate spoon at a flea market ($1 - $2).
Wrap all with cellophane and tie with a bow.

Hot Raspberry Tea
Spoonful Mix

3 tsp. sugar
2 tsp. Country Time® lemonade powder (not sugar free)
1 tsp. unsweetened instant tea
1/2 tsp. raspberry gelatin (not sugar free)

1. Mix all ingredients in small bowl.
2. Place mix into plastic wrap and attach to spoon.
   Decorate spoon. Attach instructions at top of pg. 19.
   (See pgs. 3-6 for detailed instructions on this.)

Hot Raspberry Tea

1. Remove decorative wrapping from spoon, leaving the mix inside the plastic wrap and still attached to spoon.
2. Hold spoon over a mug and cut open bag of mix, allowing mix to fall into mug.
3. Add one cup (8 oz.) boiling water.
4. Stir until well mixed. (Use gift spoon to stir!)

Hot Spiced Lemon Tea
Spoonful Mix

3 tsp. sugar
2 tsp. Country Time® lemonade powder (not sugar free)
1 tsp. unsweetened instant tea
1/4 tsp. ground ginger
1/4 tsp. ground allspice
1/4 tsp. cinnamon
1/8 tsp. ground cloves

1. Mix all ingredients in small bowl.
2. Place mix into plastic wrap and attach to spoon. Decorate spoon. Attach instructions below. (See pgs. 3-6 for detailed instructions on this.)

Hot Spiced Lemon Tea

1. Remove decorative wrapping from spoon, leaving the mix inside the plastic wrap and still attached to spoon.
2. Hold spoon over a mug and cut open bag of mix, allowing mix to fall into mug.
3. Add one cup (8 oz.) boiling water.
4. Stir until well mixed. (Use gift spoon to stir!)

Spoon Specialties

Give 6 spoonfuls of any of the drink mixes (pgs. 16 to 22) in a gift basket with some fortune cookies.

Cherry Mulling Spice
Spoonful Mix

1 tsp. Country Time® lemonade mix (not sugar free)
1 tsp. cherry gelatin mix (not sugar free)
1/4 tsp. cinnamon

1. Mix all ingredients in small bowl.
2. Place mix into plastic wrap and attach to spoon.
   Decorate spoon. Attach instructions below.
   (See pgs. 3-6 for detailed instructions on this.)

NOTE: This mix flavors: apple juice, apple cider or cranberry juice. Leave the instructions below as is to give the recipient the choice. If you want to guide them to one of the choices (like apple cider- if you are giving them a bottle of apple cider and 4 spoons of mix for example) then in instruction #3 below leave out the reference to the other choices and only say "Add one cup (8 oz.) heated apple cider."

Cherry Mulling Spice

1. Remove decorative wrapping from spoon, leaving the mix inside the plastic wrap and still attached to spoon.
2. Hold spoon over a mug and cut open bag of mix, allowing mix to fall into mug.
3. Add one cup (8 oz.) heated apple juice, apple cider or cranberry juice.
4. Stir until well mixed. (Use gift spoon to stir!)

Spoon Specialties

Give a "Winter Warmer" basket with a quart bottle of apple juice or cider (tie a bow around neck of bottle).
Include 4 Cherry Mulling Spice Spoons (one for each of the 4 cups of juice in the bottle).

Mulling Spice
Spoonful Mix

1 tsp. Country Time® lemonade mix (not sugar free)
1 tsp. sugar
1/4 tsp. cinnamon
1/4 tsp. nutmeg

1. Mix all ingredients in small bowl.
2. Place mix into plastic wrap and attach to spoon.
   Decorate spoon. Attach instructions below.
   (See pgs. 3-6 for detailed instructions on this.)

NOTE: This mix flavors any of: apple juice, apple cider, white zinfandel wine or red wine. Leave the instructions below as is to give the recipient the choice. If you want to guide them to one of the choices (like red wine- if you are giving them a bottle of wine and 4 spoons of mix for example) then in instruction #3 below leave out the reference to the other choices and only say "Add one cup (8 oz.) heated red wine."

Mulling Spice

1. Remove decorative wrapping from spoon, leaving the mix inside the plastic wrap and still attached to spoon.
2. Hold spoon over a mug and cut open bag of mix, allowing mix to fall into mug.
3. Add one cup (8 oz.) heated apple juice, apple cider, cranberry juice, white zinfandel wine or red wine.
4. Stir until well mixed. (Use gift spoon to stir!)

Spoon Specialties

Give a bottle of red wine with 4 Mulling Spice Spoons tied onto the neck of the bottle with ribbons.

Hot Spiced Chai Tea Latte
Spoonful Mix

2 1/2 tsp. vanilla flavor powdered coffee creamer
2 1/2 tsp. sugar
3/4 tsp. unsweetened instant tea
1/4 tsp. ground ginger
1/4 tsp. ground allspice
1/4 tsp. ground cloves
1/4 tsp. cinnamon

1. Mix all ingredients in small bowl.
2. Place mix into plastic wrap and attach to spoon.
   Decorate spoon. Attach instructions below.
   (See pgs. 3-6 for detailed instructions on this.)

Hot Spiced Chai Tea Latte

1. Remove decorative wrapping from spoon, leaving the
   mix inside the plastic wrap and still attached to spoon.
2. Hold spoon over a mug and cut open bag of mix, allowing
   mix to fall into mug.
3. Add 3/4 cup (6 oz.) boiling water.
4. Stir until well mixed. (Use gift spoon to stir!)

Spoon Specialties

Use a 10 to 12 oz. styrofoam cup with a lid. Cut a slit into the lid. Place Chai Mix Spoon into cup. Let spoon handle stick up through the lid. Wrap all with tissue paper or cello-phane. Tie with a bow.

Parmesan Herb
Spoonful Mix

1 Tb. Parmesan cheese (green
   can) or any Parmesan
   blend in a can
1/2 Tb. dried parsley flakes
3/4 tsp. sugar
1/2 tsp. dried minced onion

1/4 tsp. dried oregano leaves
1/4 tsp. dried thyme leaves
1/4 tsp. dried basil leaves
1/4 tsp. garlic powder
1/8 tsp. coarse ground black
   pepper

1. Mix all ingredients in small bowl.
2. Place mix into plastic wrap and attach to spoon.
   Decorate spoon. (See pgs. 3-6 for detailed instructions
   on this.) There are three recipes that can be made with
   this mix. Decide which one you want to use and attach
   instructions for that one (all are listed below).

Parmesan Herb Dip

1. Remove decorative wrapping from spoon, leaving the
   mix inside the plastic wrap and still attached to spoon.
2. Place **1/3 cup mayonnaise and 1/3 cup sour cream**
   into a medium bowl.
3. Hold spoon over bowl and cut open bag of mix, allowing
   mix to fall into bowl onto mayo and sour cream.
4. Mix until very well blended. (Use gift spoon to mix!)
   Store in refrigerator, but serve at room temp.
5. Serve with chips or raw vegetables.

Parmesan Herb Olive Oil Dip For Bread

1. Remove decorative wrapping from spoon, leaving the
   mix inside the plastic wrap and still attached to spoon.
2. Place **1/2 cup extra virgin olive oil** in medium bowl.
3. Hold spoon over bowl and cut open bag of mix, allowing
   mix to fall into bowl onto olive oil
4. Mix with a whisk until very well blended.
5. Pour into a shallow saucer to serve. Dip French or Italian
   bread pieces into this.

Parmesan Herb Pasta Butter

1. Remove decorative wrapping from spoon, leaving the
   mix inside the plastic wrap and still attached to spoon.
2. Place **1/2 stick melted butter** into a medium bowl.
3. Hold spoon over bowl and cut open bag of mix,
   allowing mix to fall into bowl onto melted butter.
4. Mix well with a whisk.
5. Toss over 6 oz. of hot cooked pasta. (Or mix seasoning with
   a stick of butter and toss over 12 oz. hot cooked pasta.)

Dill Dip
Spoonful Mix

3 tsp. dried parsley flakes
1 1/2 tsp. dried dill weed
3/4 tsp. salt free herb seasoning blend (some brands
   are Spike®, Mrs. Dash Original®, Lawry's Salt Free 17®,
   McCormick All Purpose Seasoning®).
   (Don't buy a seasoning with salt.)
3/4 tsp. sugar
pinch salt

1. Mix all ingredients in small bowl.
2. Place mix into plastic wrap and attach to spoon.
   Decorate spoon. Attach instructions below.
   (See pgs. 3-6 for detailed instructions on this.)

Dill Dip

1. Remove decorative wrapping from spoon, leaving the
   mix inside the plastic wrap and still attached to spoon.
2. Place **3/4 cup mayonnaise and 3/4 cup sour
   cream** into a medium bowl.
3. Hold spoon over bowl and cut open bag of mix, allowing
   mix to fall into bowl onto mayo and sour cream.
4. Mix until very well blended. (Use gift spoon to stir!)
   Store in refrigerator.
5. Serve with chips or raw vegetables.

Spoon Specialties

   Place several different flavors of dip spoons (pgs. 12-14
and 23-27) into a small decorative cellophane bag (crafts
store). Tie with a ribbon.

Garlic Onion Dip
Spoonful Mix

1 Tb. garlic powder
1 Tb. onion powder
1/2 Tb. dried parsley flakes
1/2 tsp. salt free herb seasoning blend (some brands
    are Spike®, Mrs. Dash Original®, Lawry's Salt Free 17®,
    McCormick All Purpose Seasoning®).
    (Don't buy a seasoning with salt.)
1 shake salt

1. Mix all ingredients in small bowl.
2. Place mix into plastic wrap and attach to spoon.
    Decorate spoon. Attach instructions below.
    (See pgs. 3-6 for detailed instructions on this.)

Garlic Onion Dip

1. Remove decorative wrapping from spoon, leaving the
    mix inside the plastic wrap and still attached to spoon.
2. Place **1 cup mayonnaise and 1 cup sour cream**
    into a medium bowl.
3. Hold spoon over bowl and cut open bag of mix, allowing
    mix to fall into bowl onto mayo and sour cream.
4. Mix until very well blended. (Use gift spoon to mix!)
    Store in refrigerator, but serve at room temperature.
5. Serve with chips and raw vegetables.

Spoon Specialties

    Place 4 to 5 decorated dip spoons into a quart jar.
Put lid on the jar. Decorate the lid of the jar to match the
decorations on the spoons.

Fiesta Dip
Spoonful Mix

1 Tb. chili powder
2 tsp. dried parsley flakes
1 tsp. sugar
1/2 tsp. garlic powder
1/2 tsp. McCormick® dried cilantro leaves
1/4 tsp. coarse black pepper
1/4 tsp onion powder
dash cayenne (red) pepper

1. Mix all ingredients in small bowl.
2. Place mix into plastic wrap and attach to spoon.
   Decorate spoon. Attach instructions below.
   (See pgs. 3-6 for detailed instructions on this.)

Fiesta Dip

1. Remove decorative wrapping from spoon, leaving the
   mix inside the plastic wrap and still attached to spoon.
2. Place **1 cup mayonnaise and 1 cup sour cream**
   into a medium bowl.
3. Hold spoon over bowl and cut open bag of mix, allowing
   mix to fall into bowl onto mayo and sour cream.
4. Mix until very well blended. (Use gift spoon to mix!)
   Store in refrigerator, but serve at room temp.
5. Serve with chips.

Spoon Specialties

Tie several Fiesta Dip Spoons (or a variety of dip spoons)
into a bandana. Tie bandana closed with thin rope or raffia.

Cajun Dip
Spoonful Mix

1 Tb. paprika
1 tsp. dried thyme leaves
1 tsp. dried oregano leaves
1 tsp. onion powder
1/2 tsp. sugar
1/2 tsp. garlic powder
1/2 tsp. cayenne (red) pepper

1. Mix all ingredients in small bowl.
2. Place mix into plastic wrap and attach to spoon.
   Decorate spoon. Attach instructions below.
   (See pgs. 3-6 for detailed instructions on this.)

Cajun Dip

1. Remove decorative wrapping from spoon, leaving the
   mix inside the plastic wrap and still attached to spoon.
2. Place **3/4 cup mayonnaise and 3/4 cup sour
   cream** into a medium bowl.
3. Hold spoon over bowl and cut open bag of mix, allowing
   mix to fall into bowl onto mayo and sour cream.
4. Mix until very well blended. (Use gift spoon to mix!)
   Store in refrigerator, but serve at room temperature.
5. Serve with chips.

Spoon Specialties

Tie a Cajun Dip Spoon onto a bag of stick pretzels.

Bacon Cheeseball
Spoonful Mix

1 1/2 Tb. finely broken McCormick® Bac 'N Pieces Bacon
    Flavored Bits
1 1/2 tsp. ranch salad dressing mix
1 tsp. dried parsley flakes

1. Place bacon bits into a sandwich bag and break them
    into fine pieces by rolling a heavy food can over them.
2. Mix all ingredients in small bowl.
3. Place mix into plastic wrap and attach to spoon.
    Decorate spoon. Attach instructions below.
    (See pgs. 3-6 for detailed instructions on this.)

Bacon Cheeseball

1. Remove decorative wrapping from spoon, leaving the
    mix inside the plastic wrap and still attached to spoon.
2. Place **1 (8 oz.) block cream cheese**, room temp-
    erature into medium bowl.
3. Hold spoon over bowl and cut open bag of mix, allowing
    mix to fall into bowl onto cream cheese.
4. Mix until very well blended. Shape into a ball.
5. Serve with crackers or raw vegetables. Store in
    refrigerator, but serve at room temperature.

Spoon Specialties

    Take an empty food can (like a green bean can). Place
4 to 5 decorated spoons in the can with the decorated ends
of the spoons sticking out of the top of the can. Use the
same decorations you used for the spoons to decorate the
can. (Use paper to make a new label for the can - tie
ribbons around the can.) Attach the recipe card for the
spoons to the outside of the can. (Cookbook Cupboard has a book
about giving cake and bread mixes in cans - see copyright page of
this book for ordering information.)

Spicy Spread
Spoonful Mix

1 1/2 Tb. salt free herb seasoning blend (some brands are Spike®, Mrs. Dash Original®, Lawry's Salt Free 17®, McCormick All Purpose Seasoning®). (Don't buy a seasoning with salt.)
2 tsp. coarse ground black pepper

1. Mix all ingredients in small bowl.
2. Place mix into plastic wrap and attach to spoon. Decorate spoon. Attach instructions below. (See pgs. 3-6 for detailed instructions on this.)

Spicy Spread

1. Remove decorative wrapping from spoon, leaving the mix inside the plastic wrap and still attached to spoon.
2. Place an **(8 oz.) block cream cheese**, room temperature, into a medium bowl.
3. Hold spoon over bowl and cut open bag of mix, allowing mix to fall into bowl onto cream cheese.
4. Mix until very well blended. Store in refrigerator, but serve at room temperature.
5. Serve with crackers or raw vegetables.

Spoon Specialties

Place 3 to 4 decorated Spicy Spread Spoons into a paper towel roll. Wrap roll with tissue, cellophane or wrapping paper that is 4" longer on each end than the roll.

Use chenille stems to tie each end of the cellophane closed. Attach recipe card to roll.

Dill Butter (or Herb Butter)
Spoonful Mix

Choose one ingredient below:

1 tsp. dried dillweed

OR 1 tsp. salt free herb seasoning blend (some brands
are Spike®, Mrs. Dash Original®, Lawry's Salt Free 17®,
McCormick All Purpose Seasoning®)
(Don't buy a seasoning with salt.)

1. Place your choice of seasoning into plastic wrap and
attach to spoon. Decorate spoon. Attach instructions
below. Name it either Dill Butter or Herb Butter
depending on which flavor you are using.
(See pgs. 3-6for detailed instructions on this.)

Dill Butter

1. Remove decorative wrapping from spoon, leaving the
mix inside the plastic wrap and still attached to spoon.
2. Place **1/2 stick butter or margarine**, room temperature, (this is 1/4 cup) into a medium bowl.
3. Hold spoon over bowl and cut open bag of mix, allowing
mix to fall into bowl onto butter.
4. Mix until very well blended.
5. Serve on hot rolls or on hot cooked vegetables.

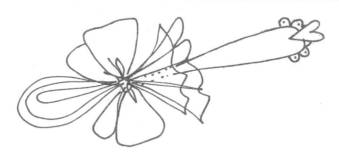

Spoon *Specialties*

Attach a matching plastic knife to the Dill Butter Spoon.
Cross the spoon and knife into an X shape. Tape them
together (the decorations on the spoon will hide the tape).
This will be the recipients "butter knife" for spreading.

Garlic Butter
Spoonful Mix

1/4 tsp. garlic powder
1/2 tsp. dried parsley flakes

1. Mix ingredients in small bowl.
1. Place mix into plastic wrap and attach to spoon. Decorate spoon. Attach instructions below. (See pgs. 3-6 for detailed instructions on this.)

Garlic Butter

1. Remove decorative wrapping from spoon, leaving the mix inside the plastic wrap and still attached to spoon.
2. Place **1/2 stick butter or margarine**, room temperature (this is 1/4 cup) into a medium bowl.
3. Hold spoon over bowl and cut open bag of mix, allowing mix to fall into bowl onto butter.
4. Mix until very well blended.
5. Spread generously on bread slices and broil until lightly toasted. Or spread in between slices of a French bread loaf. Wrap loaf in foil and heat 30 minutes at 350°

Spoon Specialties

Attach a Garlic Butter Mix to a wooden spoon instead of a plastic spoon. Cover bowl of wooden spoon with calico fabric. Tie fabric onto spoon with raffia. The recipient uses the wooden spoon to mix the garlic butter.

Ranch Dressing
Spoonful Mix

2 tsp. dried parsley flakes
1 tsp. salt free herb seasoning blend (some brands
    are Spike®, Mrs. Dash Original®, Lawry's Salt Free 17®,
    McCormick All Purpose Seasoning®).
    (Don't buy a seasoning with salt.)
1/2 tsp. garlic powder
1/4 tsp. dried basil leaves

1. Mix all ingredients in small bowl.
2. Place mix into plastic wrap and attach to spoon.
   Decorate spoon. Attach instructions below.
   (See pgs. 3-6 for detailed instructions on this.)
   This is a good mix to give in a wooden spoon -
   they can use the spoon to mix the dressing and
   to serve the salad.

Ranch Dressing

1. Remove decorative wrapping from spoon, leaving the
   mix inside the plastic wrap and still attached to spoon
2. Empty **1/2 cup mayonnaise and 1/2 cup buttermilk** into a medium bowl.
3. Hold spoon over bowl and cut open bag of mix, allowing
   mix to fall into bowl onto mayo and buttermilk.
4. Mix until very well blended. (Use gift spoon to mix!)
   Refrigerate 30 minutes up to 8 hours to blend flavors.

Index